Borrowed Towns

Borrowed Towns

Richard Newman

Word Press

Published by Word Press
P.O. Box 541106
Cincinnati, OH 45254-1106

Typeset in Dutch by WordTech Communications LLC,
Cincinnati, OH

ISBN: 1933456019
LCCN: 2005927729

Poetry Editor: Kevin Walzer
Business Editor: Lori Jareo

Visit us on the web at www.word-press.com

Cover photograph by John Hilgert (1956-2002): "Untitled"
(Carmi, Illinois, 1996), courtesy the estate of John Hilgert

Acknowledgments

Grateful acknowledgment is made to the following magazines where these poems first appeared:

American Literary Review: "Funeral Procession"
Big Muddy: "Salem, Indiana, 1983"
Black Dirt: "Gum Gatherers"
Boulevard: "Burial," "Crawlspace," "Fireflies," "Grampa's Liquor Bottles"
Crab Orchard Review: "Box Trap," "Briefcase of Sorrow," "Coins"
Delmar: "Eliot's Pig," "Tastes Like Chicken"
5AM: "Mothra"
Margie: "Bigfoot," "River Thing"
The Melic Review: "Vampire Laments the Loss of His Reflection"
Meridian: "Crossing Schlensker Ditch"
Natural Bridge: "Sandy's Grave," "Stripper Pits," "Under Your Bed"
Poems & Plays: "Mistakes," "Wild Game"
River Styx: "Ash"
Seattle Review: "December Evening"
Slant: "River Revisited"
Southern Humanities Review: "For the Taking"
Southern Indiana Review: "In the Olden Days"
Southern Poetry Review: "Pink Palace"
Sou'wester: "Life After Prison"
Spoon River Poetry Review: "Highway Sounds," "Phantoms"
The Sun: "Mowing"
Sundog: The Southeast Review: "Reject"
Tar River Poetry: "Back at Sportsman's Den Pool Hall"
The Virtual Word: "Slow Fires"

Some of these poems appeared in the following anthologies: "Salem, Indiana, 1983" in *Like Thunder: Poets Respond to Violence in America* (University of Iowa Press); "Fireflies" and "Grandpa's Liquor Bottles" in *Memoirs and Memory: Essays, Poems, Stories, and Letters by Contemporary Missouri Authors* (The Mid-America Press); "Pink Palace" in *3-Chord Poems* (Deep Cleveland Press); "Theology" in *Vespers: Contemporary American Poems of Religion and Spirituality* (University of Iowa Press). Many of these poems also appeared in the chapbooks *Monster Gallery: 19 Terrifying and Amazing Monster Sonnets!* (Snark Publications, 2005), *Tastes Like Chicken and Other Meditations* (Snark Publications, 2004) and *Greatest Hits* (Pudding House Press, 2001).

Special thanks to Eric Baggett, Richard Burgin, The Cat's Meow, Richard Cecil, Amy Clark, The Food Group, Albert Goldbarth, Andrew Hudgins, Indian buffet, Joanne Lowery, Fishstix McQueen, Betsy Millard and Mark Tyler, Kara Moyer, Molly Peacock, River Styxers past and present, Carrie Robb, Catie Rosemurgy, Jeanie Thompson, Uncle Larry, The Wednesday Club of Saint Louis, Tom Wilhelmus, all my drinking buddies and hoop pals and Spalding compadres, and, of course, my mother, my father, Natalie, and Otis.

For my family, both living and long dead

Whether all towns and all who live in them
Are more or less the same, I leave to you.

—Edwin Arlington Robinson, "Tasker Norcross"

And even though the next country is so close
that people can hear its roosters crowing
and its dogs barking,
they are content to die of old age
without ever having gone to see it.

—Lao-Tsu, *The Tao Te Ching*

Contents

3. Phantoms

1. Gift of Idle Hours

Coins

My change: a nickel caked with finger grime;
two nicked quarters not long for this life, worth
more for keeping dead eyes shut than bus fare;
a dime, shining in sunshine like a new dime;
grubby pennies, one stamped the year of my birth,
no brighter than I from 40 years of wear.

What purses, piggy-banks, and window sills
have these coins known, their presidential heads
pinched into what beggar's chalky palm—
they circulate like tarnished red blood cells,
all of us exchanging the merest film
of our lives, and the lives of those long dead.

And now my turn in the convenience store,
I hand over my fist of change, still warm,
to the bored, lip-pierced check-out girl, once more
to be spun down cigarette machines, hurled
in fountains, flipped for luck—these dirty charms
chiming in the dark pockets of the world.

Crossing Schlensker Ditch

Between Schlensker Ditch and Bosch Ditch
on 41 South, between brown fields, where
in *North by Northwest* the crop duster chased
Cary Grant over brittle corn stubble,
where rusty fences slouch drunkenly
into a gray horizon, a scrawl of trees—
home is a land that offers no return.
Hitchcock picked it for its stunning bleakness.
Even the long band of blackbirds, thick
as gnats and stretching over a hundred acres,
reluctantly touches down here and there
to pick through a few splintered kernels
then slowly billows over the highway, south,
to leave this area so lost, so lacking
monuments the people name the ditches.
The only populations that increase
are cemetery, prison, and hog factory.
A few miles north, Santa Claus Land crumbles
back to meadow. Barns collapse slow-motion.
Abandoned trailers snooze along dirt roads.
My young daughter and I also migrate
for the holiday, muttering our thanks
we no longer live here in Gibson County,
picking over a dead bird's bones,
picking through the best of my childhood
as we leave with boxes of books and games,
a few pictures, a tuneless ukulele,
and as we finally head back home, due west,
returning to this land who knows when,
the wind finds a small opening in the car,
its long finger pricking under my skin.

Mowing

Sitting quietly, doing nothing,
Spring comes, and the grass grows by itself.

—classic Zen poem from the *Zenrin Kushu*

I'm no Buddhist, but I know enough of lawns
to say the grass grows by itself even
when I'm not sitting quietly. Take now,
for example: I'm in a terrible mood, full
of so much desire and April cruelty
I could wash away the four noble truths,
and, almost as I mow, the new growth
pushes against my chloroplasted shoes.
Even as a child visiting Virginia,
I gazed down picnic-perfect battlefields
and guessed that before the last cannonballs
burst and the last dying soldiers cried
their mothers' names into the air, the grass
was already swarming back up the bloody hills,
as it now goes about its green business
with entrepreneurial zeal, cracking sidewalks
and dishevelling my brick patio.
And when my daughter swings in our back yard,
crying, "Watch me, Daddy! Look how high!"
I look up from the mower as she launches
into the leafy arms of the trees, the whole
swingset heaving, then swoops back down again,
her bare feet riffling over the blades,
grass I scattered with my own two fists,
and I know—sitting, standing, quiet or not—
that as she grows there's nothing I can do.

Shadows

We flit in corners of your eyes
and vanish when you turn to look,
faster than the black crow flies.
You strain over your open book
through dying light to make us out—
those childish hopes you haven't snuffed?
A forgotten little flock of doubts?
A pack of qualms, B-movie stuff,
dark secrets and their trains of guilt,
the luckless spirit of a dead friend?
Turn off the light, crawl under a quilt—
we lie in wait for the day to end
and take the shapes that you presume
when cast like night across your room.

Ash

for John Hilgert

With your cock-eyed rhythm you couldn't play your way
out of a 12-bar blues with your eyes closed,
so we'd strum a minute and spend the rest of the night
sighing and telling lies. Drowsy from pot roast,
we'd sprawl across the back porch and guzzle
Rolling Rocks like children eat chocolate,
though even then you complained of stomach pains,
and though I'd smoke a pack of cigarettes,
you would be the one we'd lose to cancer.
One night my backyard neighbor built a bonfire,
burning what must have been a decade's worth
of newspapers and phonebooks, who knows what—
wedding pictures, love letters? In a month
he'd sell his house and move. "Gee,"
you said, "that must feel really really good."
We watched his silhouette stalking back and forth,
tossing more and more things onto the fire,
each time sending up a fountain of sparks
blinking orange then drifting over the fence
into our yard, winking out and whitening
as they fluttered to us and settled on the porch
like a flock of grizzled gulls, a silent ash-storm.
We breathed and tasted ash, and you lay peppered
and unperturbed, an empty on your chest.
"You asleep?" I wondered. "No," you said,
"just taking in the night. And your neighbor's past.
But I wouldn't mind another beer." Inside,
I scrounged another stale cigarette,
bleeped the messages from my own ex-wife

("Who cares," you'd say, "she'll still be pissed tomorrow.")
and grabbed a few more beers for each of us,
but back out on the porch I found you gone,
drawn to the dying fire like a moth
or child, pushing your way through leafy greens,
my dogwoods, further into the dark. Below me,
the whole porch mottled in white and gray except
the blank space where your body had lain, your outline
in ash, and you, covered in the ashen remains
of what can only cling to us, the living.

Briefcase of Sorrow

*"Some writers get into the habit of letting of name a
metaphor without really showing the image to the reader:
sea of life, mattress of the soul, river of death . . . or (perhaps
the worst) briefcase of sorrow."*

—Frances Mayes, *The Discovery of Poetry*

My briefcase of sorrow slumps by the door.
The semester's done. I leave it behind,
all my manila folders of grief (stacked
and alphabetized, bound with rubber bands
of stretched hope), pens of overachievement,
and pencils of petty angst. At some point,
I suppose I should dump its insides out
on the table, the staple remover
of apocalypse, a few sticky notes
of indecision. Poor briefcase—it can't
ingest them, try as it may, and I should
especially purge the gradebook of mixed
endeavors, the crumbs of last month's sandwich.
Not now. My neighborhood pub calls louder
than some cloying briefcase, strap of pity
wagging as I leave, its two bright buckles
of expectation gleaming for my return
once again, when I will spill its contents,
the paperclips of despair, the Wetnaps
of desire, bringing it, light and swinging,
along my side to fill one more time its
compartment of everything and nothing.

The Beast in Me

isn't savage but a clod, dumb bumbler,
winces at the harm he never meant you,
sits on the back porch at night and howls
at the radio tower and by day flinches
at your make and model and color on the road
though you are 900 miles away, blurts
bone-headed thoughts then gnaws on them for days,
loves you, isn't vicious but naïve,
believes everything you tell him about me,
wants to lick your wounds, lick you everywhere
down to your inner beast, set it free
to stumble over oafish fields, paw
in padded paw, before they sink their claws
once again into our ripened hearts.

Fireflies

Tonight my yard is full of fireflies—
a glitterfest of green, blinking by hundreds,
exactly like last year, when she and I
drove out into the Missouri countryside
to talk about our marriage. It was thick
with greenery. The air was hot and thick,
and we had decided to try and stay together,
though by first light she'd changed her mind again,
and, to be honest, our eleventh hour
hope and promise lacked the weight of truth.
We wandered off the rocky dirt road
over weeds and brambles, through branches
and spiderwebs, and pressed into a clearing,
and it was like a pocket in the darkness
that surrounded us—the misty night
backlit with thousands of glittering fireflies
bettering the stars. It was a mating dance,
and we gazed into a sputtering green sea
of desire—such irresistible beckoning.
Ours was, too—a death-dance of mating,
a slower, indecisive tarantella,
and she asked me never to write about this,
but I knew then that I had nothing to lose,
that at that moment there was nothing I wanted
more than to write about the fireflies.

Vampire Laments the Loss of His Reflection

Unlife is difficult when you're a dandy
and can't register the faintest reflection.
Pre-undead days, nothing came nearer perfection
than my mirror—me, my own eye-candy.
Ah, how I brought the drabbest puddle to life.
My surface outshone on a given summer day
the classiest Marshall-Fields window display.
I'd fix a misplaced hair in the butter knife.
Now, though I am ageless, I grow old,
invisible as death. I'm left to seek
in my victims' eye the beauty they behold
before I suck the rosy from their lips,
devour the apple-redness from their cheeks,
and drain them down to their wilted fingertips.

Theology

"I don't believe in God but gravity,"
my father told me, tossing a clod of earth
down the canyon. An arm around my shoulder,
the other sweeping the western panorama,
he said, "This is all too big for God,"
and pared my religious education down
to two subjects: nature and hard work.
I rarely saw him except for those vacations
crammed with hiking, backpacking, cross-country
skiing, tennis, body-surfing, rock-climbing,
and then he'd return to his 80-hour weeks,
days beginning at four or five a.m.
for forty years, and finally he retired
to unwrap his unwanted gift of idle hours
in a little cabin in the Colorado Rockies,
where if I call I'll find him hammering
up on the roof, among the pine, kneeling
on shingles, each tiny echo of his labor
a kiss against the endless blue sky.

December Evening

A shitty day at work, I come home tired
to fix dinner for my hungry daughter:
the fastest—mac & cheese. I boil the water,
look out the kitchen window at phone wires
cutting across the sky, gray and thick
as curdled milk, the rows and rows of boarded
up homes, the brewery chimneys blowing sordid
smells, the alley piles of scabby bricks,
a landscape so man-made it's inhumane.
On many evenings such as these I've thought
how only when we're too tired and strained
to feel it can we truly call it love,
and so I drain the noodles, return the pot
to the orange coils of sunset on my stove.

2. Bottomlands

Grampa's Liquor Bottles

Stiff in our black funeral ties and jackets,
my brother and I crept out the kitchen door,
escaping the crowded family room, far
from the somber drone of voices and Grampa,
hands positioned on his motionless chest.
We crossed the yard, went straight for the corncrib,
and nosing behind a cobweb-covered plow
we found a row of bottles—ancient bottles,
green, and when held to the light, glazed with dust.
We lined them up along the window ledge,
and from the other side of the barn threw rocks,
most landing in the green sea of cornstalks
beginning to brown in the late July heat.
Before long we remembered our 22's,
nearly forgot the funeral inside.
We took turns exploding the thick green glass,
wondered aloud if Grampa would get buried
with his false teeth in or if they'd stay
in that bathroom jar, magnified forever
to the size of horse teeth. The bottles shattered as if
from inside themselves, sides bursting out, necks
toppling over, and suddenly Dad was there,
standing beside us. Our hearts jumped with fear,
our faces braced for rage. What happened next
mystified us, because it was Dad's dad
that lay dead inside, and because of that death
we came to the family farm, full of grieving
strangers and unfamiliar family members,
and Dad stood almost unrecognizable
next to the disused corncrib, his face pale,
so pale in the morning shade, and expressionless.

"Make sure you pick up every piece of glass,"
was all he said and headed back to the house,
sparing us our awkward imitations
of grief and letting us get back to the work
of boys with mercifully protracted childhoods.
We lay down our guns and lined another row
of Grampa's liquor bottles under the sun,
let them fill with light one last time
and glow with phosphorescent life, and then
we shot them to slivers in the oily black dirt.

Box Trap

Grampa broke the wooden slats
and catfish spilled on the creekbank,
a pool of wriggling mud, cornmeal,
fins, and twitching whiskers. He tied
his homemade trap to the twisted steel
and cement remnants of a bridge
now washed from the muddy bend
where every year the current cuts
a foot from the bank, the back forty.
And Grampa said, "If the game warden
came he'd break the box open,
kick the fish back in the creek.
The trap takes too many, you see."
I watched him nail a row of fish
across a long board and hatchet
off the heads, several dozen,
enough even for all the cousins,
and the heads stared in the long grass,
the smell calling farmcats for miles,
while the row of headless fish curled
and uncurled against the nails
like they were doing exercises.
I wish that I could say I remember
tasting the sweet white flesh,
the extended family laughing together,
jubilant up and down the table.
Or the opposite, that I couldn't swallow
the bitter taste of brack and mire
and my grandfather cheating the creek.
But I can't. All that I remember
is the row of headless fish

still flexing after half an hour,
their taste vanished like the last time
I visited the creekbank by the bridge—
gone—twenty feet of rich,
black earth sliced off and dissolved
into that fishless, muddy current.

Wild Game

When my great grandma Lizzie moved to town,
her husband promptly sent her to finishing school—
for none of the dainty china or fancy jewels,
house full of servants or elaborate evening gowns
smoothed her backwoods edges or prettied her mouth,
its vocabulary rich in profanity.
She circled higher circles, flattered their vanity,
but kept the dishes that made her famous in the south:

raccoon in barberry sauce, Grand Pacific Game
Pie (with woodcock or snipe), herb-roasted otter,
Spanish fricasseed rabbit garnished with roses.
It wasn't that her wildness was tamed—
Lizzie used the finishing they taught her
to sneak the savagery in under their noses.

Roast haunch of venison, roast possum
with cranberry sauce, hare pie, quail on toast
points, merckle turtle stew, and the most
famous dish of all: cherry blossom
gravy, dumplings, and beer-battered squirrel.
But even when she cooked domesticated
fare, she made it game. Neighbors hated
to watch her grab a backyard hen, twirl

it over her head, and with a snap of the wrist
launch the headless bird into the air—
to land veering like a top too tightly wound
and raining a trail of blood on the dry ground.
And though its comb went limp, the eyes would stare
accusingly from Lizzie's bloodied fist.

Eliot's Pig

Eliot's pig was a demon-pig.
We found this out one night when it crossed
the barbed wires, plunged down and up
the creek bank, trampled the briars
and scraggly creek willows to clatter
the back porch cat dishes and wipe his nose
on Ralph Edson's sliding glass door.

And we all laughed at how that pig
must have scared poor Ralph off his couch
in a rumpus of clothes, want-ads, and month-old
cereal bowls and sent him into the night,
swaying on his back porch in the blue
light of his TV set for some time
before he decided not to shoot.

The next morning we found Eliot's pig
plopped in the shade of Ralph Edson's
broken down riding mower that he ran
hard into a tree once and left there
to rust ever since, and it was all
the four of us could do (Ralph, Eliot,
Bernie Webster with his oversized snowshovel,
and myself) to get that pig in Eliot's truck.

Its people-eyes looked up at us, angry
and bored, as we chased it on Ralph's weedy
lawn and through the overgrown hedges,
and finally we got him halfway up the plank
and he just stopped there, not even looking at us,
until Bernie Webster swatted his ass

and he stepped in the truck bed and lay down.

And when that demon-pig showed up again
a few days later in Ralph's backyard,
Ralph didn't seem to mind, probably threw him
scraps of TV dinners or Hamburger Helper,
let him forage the wild onions and black walnuts
and muddy the earth so Ralph wouldn't need
to mow for a long time, if ever.

And Eliot sure took his time getting that pig,
before he guessed this is how it's going to be,
and drove it 15 miles into Toulon
for slaughter. And now, the middle of fall,
we drive past the Edson place with no
grass, skeletons of shrubbery, and this year's
black walnuts devoured hulls and all,
and that riding mower like a rusted
sundial, its shadow stretching
longer and longer over Ralph Edson's
trampled waste of a backyard.

Tastes Like Chicken

Quail, pheasant, goose you might expect,
but froglegs, rabbit, squirrel, rattlesnake—
these things, too, I promise, taste like chicken.
And if you like the taste of chicken, try
the llama or the alligator soup,
terrapin creek turtle or roasted dove.
Don't be intimidated by strange game
or kangaroo or wild stir-fried dog.
More often than not, most things taste like chicken.
But one thing you might think tastes like chicken,
at least a very big chicken, is ostrich,
which actually doesn't taste like chicken at all,
but tastes like steak, or maybe a filet mignon.
Your small game birds—plover, thrush, lark,
snipe, and woodcock—taste like chicken. Partridge
tastes like chicken. Muskrat tastes like chicken,
and a lot of things you wouldn't even guess:
the sweetness of success or bitter failure,
a savory victory or a bloody vengeance,
that special yearn for lost childhood, family
roots, and what you'd call the zest of life—
all compare closely to the taste of chicken.
And yes, I know what you're about to say:
that even though it's all chicken, the secret
lies in the infinite ways we can prepare it.
Let me remind you that any way you cut
through countless recipes and endless sauce,
it all boils down to the basic chicken,
clucking over this entire chickenshit world,
more common than trees and good, black dirt.
After all, we *made* the chicken, bred it,

adjusted it to the human taste bud—
the bare standard we now hold to nature.
So you better learn to like the taste of chicken,
and more important than that, its aftertaste,
which you may belch up again and again
from that unsettling soup deep in your belly.

For the Taking

Down in the mud valley,
out in the back flats,
an engine in full throttle
tears through the thick, green
cornstalks, its high-pitched
whine slapping in echo
against the bluffs. Someone
is whirring up the dust,
yellow smoke billowing
off the dirt road.
Someone is making a getaway.
Someone loves Jesus
on the back of a rusty
Dodge, making off
with a trunkload of field corn.

Our station wagon stops
beside their car. Mom leans
her head into the heat.
"May I help you?" she asks.
"The owner said I could
fill up my trunk with corn,"
he says, stacking the unripe
ears in neat rows.
The man's wife gazes
into her lap. Red soda-
mouthed kids stare
from torn-up seats, and flies
hum through open windows.
"*I'm* the owner," Mom laughed,
"and nobody asked *me*."

"Well, I talked to somebody
who farms this land, and *he*
said I could fill my trunk."

The dust from the hatchback settles,
and the station wagon sits
cock-eyed in the dirt road,
the front end sloping down
in one worn groove, like
a small white schooner tossed
in a sea of unripe cornstalks.
"Why did they want this corn,
Mom? Don't they know
this corn is grown for pigs?"
"I guess some people don't know
any better," she says. "Some people
think all corn is the same."
At the dinner table that night
we laugh, telling, retelling,
the sweet corn kernels stuck
between our teeth, despite
working and working our tongues.

Crawlspace

Our parents didn't think that we were home,
but squatting among the dirt and mouse turds
and daddylonglegs of those concrete catacombs,
my brother and I heard every single word,
heard them utter for the first time "divorce,"
such a racket like the wrath of Our Lord,
voices lashing, barging, broken, then hoarse,
footsteps pounding on the wooden floorboards
that from our side were spiked with rusty nails
twisting in flashlight beams. They'd always love us,
they said later, though at the time we couldn't exhale,
like the whole house was coming down on top of us.
But we hunkered down, refused to take flight.
Nothing could have dragged us into daylight.

Stripper Pits

Dad and I stood on the lip of the strip mine—
a mile-long black rectangular box
of a hole, like a vast burnt-out basement—
and here he explained sexual reproduction,
as if all ten-year-old boys come here,
riding bicycles through browning cornfields,
distancing broken barns and the city dump,
to press kick stands into the soft dirt
and contemplate the mechanics of the sex act.
We peered into the opened vein of blackness.
A few years later, Dad would bail me out
of trouble when the first girl I screwed got
pregnant. He knew exactly what to do.
A few years more, his marriage would fail—perhaps
for the same reason mine did—I don't know—
we resist the sticky details of Mom and Dad
as they feign virginal ignorance to ours,
all of our many infidelities—
and I've deemed my own marriage unfathomable,
growing stranger and stranger the farther distance
and forgetfulness carry me from that odd "I do."
The path inside was labyrinthian,
snaking around huge dirt piles
and ponds, those small oily reservoirs
of myth and half-truth, black waters
supposedly filled with piranhas once kept
as pets but now too large and dumped here.
Some said alligators and rabid dogs.
It was summer. The sky was blue, the ground black.
He talked in measured tones, as if the act
and all of sex and love were as simple

41

as changing a bicycle tire, and then, with an arm
around my shoulder, helped me down the switchbacks,
down into the humid darkness of the pits.

Burial

Less than a week after they found Grandpa
dead in the field beside his idling tractor,
an awful wail woke my grandma up—

an otherworldly cry like a struck child,
like her own still-born child caterwaulling
across the grave in the middle of the night—

and she never did get back to sleep, alone
in that double bed, the farmhouse a chorus
of creaks and shudders, the outside deathly still.

The next day was the first day of school,
and after mustering the resolve to teach
the first weeks, despite her husband's death,

she pushed herself into the morning light
and saw the cat impaled on her car antenna,
apparently having jumped out the hayloft,

then sunk midway down the metal rod,
hanging there dead like a flag at half mast.
Farm cats are nameless and belong to nobody,

making leftover rounds from porch to porch,
but for no reason one of Grandma's neighbors
singled this cat out and named him José,

and Grandma, who hated to squander an hour of grief
since her husband's death, couldn't bring
herself to touch the dead, stiffening creature,

and so she drove the fifteen miles to school
with José bobbing back and forth at every
bump and stop of the road, dead legs dangling,

and pulled into the parking lot, crowded
with first-day students and teachers, José waving
like a banner of death and ridiculousness,

which the janitor slowly lifted off, leaving
the antenna sticky and red and stuck with hairs
and later wiped with a rag like a rapier

in a pirate movie after he took the cat
and tossed it as unceremoniously
as possible in the dumpster in back of the school,

and which Grandma's fourth-graders found, of course,
though no one ever told her, and dissected it
like they never got to do in her science class,

probing past the delicate ribs and lungs
until they found its heart, which they left on a stump
for a sky burial of shining crows and flies.

Eye on the Sparrow, Hand on the Hog

Their bored people-eyes blink away the hours.
Lying in the shade still as tombstones,
there's nothing under the sun they won't devour:

leftover pork chops, potatoes, cauliflower
with cheese sauce; pizza with extra provolone,
their hungry eyes blinking away the hours;

fresh farm dead—a chicken overpowered
then abandoned by a fox—feathers, beak, bones
and all. There's nothing at all they won't devour.

As piglets, castrated long before their flower,
the mother wolfs up testicles—or they eat their own,
wet eyes blinking away the flies and hours.

An old farmer was similarly scoured.
They found his gold Rolex ticking—it shone
through mud, one thing beneath the sun not devoured.

We birthed and bred these creatures. They are ours,
suckling our slop till fat and fully grown,
and when at last they meet their bloody hour
there's nothing wasted, nothing not devoured.

Life after Prison

It was the deathly smell that drove us back,
staked out poor John and his property, and the closest
we could come was the weathered gatepost,
expressing our sympathy with a jar of preserves
or sometimes just a friendly wave or "Ho John,"
like we did in better days, before the war,
before misfortune bit hold and wouldn't shake loose.
He was one of Illinois' "Fighting Irish"—
newly immigrated, found a wife
and started a family and his own forty acres,
then they marched him south of the Mason-Dixon.
Before his first year of fighting, the rebels
quashed his regiment and marched him further south
to Andersonville, fenced in elbow to elbow
with nothing but feces and disease, some stale bread,
a throng of faded blues milling in the sun,
blinking away the horror and disbelief.
But John was a tall, broad-shouldered woodsman
and survived three Andersonville summers
chopping wood for extra rations, his will
unbent by hunger, humiliation, and the hot sun.
When he finally came back home, he dreamed of prison,
and before he learned to wake up knowing
he was where he was supposed to be, in bed
with his wife, the children sleeping in the next room,
the cancer began to eat into his face.
It was as if the sun, not laying him flat
in all those years of chopping wood in prison,
had bored into his fair skin like a weevil
chewing ruddy flesh down to cheekbone
and opened his skull to see what made him tick.

It grew from a small blotch into a sore,
layer after rotting layer peeling back,
his copper beard crusted with yellow pus,
his wife tearfully moving to her parents
because of the insistent stench of decay,
and in a few months you could peer into his jaw,
a row of brackish teeth gritting in agony.
I might have given anything to know
what kept that man alive, what a person
could live for after three years in prison,
an excruciating hole, and no family,
and shortly after his wife and kids moved out,
we began to hear again the rhythmic chopping,
the chop, chop, chop all day long
and into the night, like a savage clock
echoing in the flats and off the bluffs.
And then one day it stopped, and so I came
to the weathered gatepost and there was a note
tucked inside a wheelbarrow full of wood:
"My axe is had it. Here is a dollar
and a bunch of wood in fair exchange for another."
And sure enough there was a grubby dollar,
and I went myself and bought him a brand new axe.
When the chopping stopped again, we all knew.
We dug his grave first, and six of us
leaned into the stench toward his house,
with cloths stretched over our scrunched faces.
Only after he was covered with earth
did we go back up to that neglected house
to look at what he'd done—purposeful stacks
upon stacks of wood tumbling down the backyard
and reaching all the way to the edge of the forest—
enough to keep the whole community warm

long after the next approaching winter.
"Had he gone mad?" one of us asked aloud.
The chips alone kindled stoves for a year.
Someone else said maybe he thought it would save him,
since all that chopping got him through Andersonville,
but John was never any good at lying,
let alone to himself. No, it was his will,
an inability to give up his life
that drove him to chopping wood again.
It occupied his pain, but more than that,
it was the need to feel every last strain
of muscle fiber, to suck in every last
maple-, oak-, and walnut-tinged breath of air
between each solid tick and tock of his axe.
You find people like this in the world sometimes.
Often they trample the rest of us, ruthlessly.
Sometimes they try to apologize for it,
as if that will to live is a self-indulgence,
and so they try to give something back, a gift
that lasts a cold winter, then burns down
and disappears back to where it came from—
a frozen field, a white impassive sky.

Bigfoot

Life is difficult when you don't exist.
Sometimes, deep in the snowy woods, I feel
so full of life I stop to check my wrist:
nothing. But I keep on, dig in big heels,
making my fake tracks and leaving false clues.
I once tore deer-crossing signs into confetti—
it went unnoticed. I compete for front-page news
with aliens, pop-stars, Nessy, and the Yeti.
Though tabloid space is tough to get these days,
you never let me die, forever seeing
what's not there. You human beings always
believe you can believe me into being.
You analyze a hair or sift through feces,
straining to find the ghost that haunts your species.

In the Olden Days

The world held no color but sepia.
Our bedside tables creaked beneath the weight
of daily hardships, buffered only by doilies.
We did without, did things by hand. We got more
snow. Our Mickey Mouse was far from cute.
We specialized in quaint and quirky phrases
like "23 Skidoo." Our songs rang dark
with forced joy and naiveté: "Ain't We Got Fun?"
Staring from family photographs, we look
older than we are. Even as children, our faces
are shadowed with doubt and parental disappointment,
as if to say to those looking years from now:
We persist. We persevere. We do this for you.

3. Phantoms

Highway Sounds

We live so close to the highway it sounds
like we've only stopped through in a Super 8,
and I can almost feel the backdraft buckling
that cheap hotel drywall. This is how
the highway breathes: every day at rush-hour,
the wif-wif-wif of traffic, like panting,
and at night, the slow breathing of a semi
stretching across the pavement like a sigh.
Late, we lie awake talking again
after not talking all week, and listening
to traffic's constant slushing sounds of leaving
that never leave. *Where will we go?* we ask.
Who cares? we say, *so long as it's somewhere
beautiful.* But we have no money to move.
Besides, you say, *I don't think we're ready
to live together in splendid isolation.*
The sirens howl and whine throughout the night.
The traffic pulls at our hearts as we talk about
the beautiful places we might one day inhabit:
New Zealand, New Mexico, Alsace-Lorraine,
and tonight's pick, the beaches of Belize.
Our best relocation plans are conceived
after we make up from the worst fights,
and tonight is no exception, talking until
you fall asleep in mid-sentence, halfway
between here and somewhere beautiful,
where one day we hope to find ourselves,
where we will likely have far less to say,
your breathing regular now as distant waves.

River Revisited

I left town to get you out of my mind.
I knew no other way, but now I've returned
after good, distancing years to wind
the path alone among the scrubs and ferns
of the Ohio mudbanks. Talking, talking,
always talking, we were working things out,
working ourselves out, like splinters, talking about
us talking too much about us, then walking
this path. On the radio tower, the same lights blink,
the same barges churn waves to the shore.
I can't remember why I held you so fast,
resisted letting go. Each time I think
of you, I muddy the waters a little more.
You can never step twice into the same past.

Mistakes

Coach called them learning experiences,
and we sucked them up like dirt does rain, the fistfights
and pregnancies. Alvin, the smartest kid in school,
got drunk on margarita he stole from Chi-Chi's
and drove his hatchback into the Ohio River.
We were parched for learning.
                              When we grew older,
we made more learning experiences, ended up
divorced, in rehab, in jail. Now, our shoulders
stooped with learning, faces creased with experience,
we stand on the concrete bank where Alvin drowned
and try to think of what we learned. You can
never drive into the same river twice?

But it's easy to call the game from shore or sideline.
Even when we were losing, Coach would always
give the scrubs a shot at learning experience,
a chance to play and get chewed out next practice.
I was a scrub, and my name has never carried
the same thrill as when the coach picked it
out from our line of hopeless benchwarmers
and tossed me into the roiling experience,
heedless of whether I learned anything or not.

Back at Sportsman's Den Pool Hall

The barmaid who won seven million dollars
in the Indiana lottery still slides pitchers
across the bar, her mouth more creased with scowling,
her mustache a little fuller. I recognize
no one any longer, but they might as well
be the same people—the drunk couple
in the booth, her passed out against the wall,
one eye open wide and staring like
a fish on ice, him face flat on the table,
one hand still clutching a half-empty mug.
There's a whole new crop of beer-reddened faces.
Even the obscenity written about me
lies buried under generations of graffiti.
The old gang is gone, those failed conspirators—
not one of these young fucks remembers
the awful things we did, all the women
we went through like Mrs. Royster's tulips,
the right corner pocket I filled with puke.
Swig the last of the local watery beer.
Set the glass down firmly on the counter.
Wink and smile at the Mustached Lady.
It's someone else's time to be an asshole.

Gum Gatherers

Spackling knives in hand we schlepped from room
to room, overturning every desk
and scraping off the hardened little wads—
the oldest pieces tumbling like gaudy pebbles
into our five-gallon buckets, the newest
pulling off the desks in sugary strands.
For summer jobs that year we enlisted
in the school corporation, in maintenance,
but they assigned us every piece of gum
under every desk in every room
in every school in the whole school district,
then handed us our nametags, which we embellished:
Matt (guitar, vocals) and me (bass, vocals).
Our drummer had already graduated.
Most time we spent in the cafeterias,
where we overturned the long, heavy tables
jammed with a hundred different shades of gum—
pink, blue, green, and white, with an occasional
orange or purple standing out from the wads
of what looked like heaps of fossilized fungus.
Halfway into the summer we collected
our buckets: 40 gallons of spent sorbitol,
hardened spit, teenage tedium and sass,
and doubtless some of it was ours, too,
lumped in among the sexual braggadocio,

the existential angst, the rock star dreams,
tirades against the senseless institutions,
and railing against the world we didn't make
or even so much as choose to be born in,
and we dropped it, one by one, bucket and all,
into the dumpster, glad, at least for the moment,
to have gotten it all out of our systems.

Sandy's Grave

We didn't merely dance on Sandy's grave.
We revelled on it, matted down the daisies,
scattered it with cans and cigarette butts,
and draped our soggy condoms on his tombstone.
We brought along acoustic guitars and bongos
and serenaded him those summer nights,
six still-settling feet beneath us,
with endless versions of "Long Gone Sandy Blues,"
a verse for every time the straight-A student
knocked us on our asses in the crowded halls,
for every textbook scattered down the stairs,
a verse for constant taunting, fat lips, and thumps
on the backs of heads from the guy the football team
reluctantly voted "Most Valuable,"
and the stadium they renamed after him
to commemorate the place he died one practice,
a verse for each daily eulogy
delivered over the high school P.A.
("We lost the best our school had to offer.
When you think 'school spirit,' think of Sandy.")
and a verse for every mandatory minute
of those fifteen minute silent prayers,
a verse for every dubious sob and tear,
the girls' faces streaked with mascara
like double skid marks down that highway
we only wanted to leave far behind,
and best of all a night of drunken verses
for that time in physics, days after he died,
when the substitute read his name off the roll,
looked at his empty seat, asked "Where's Sandy?"
and the queasiness seeped into the room. Students

murmured down their chins and in their laps,
and she asked again, "Well, does anyone know?"
and I shamelessly raised my hand and said "He's dead,"
and she said, "That's not funny. What if something
terrible really did happen to Sandy?"
My friend looked her right in the eyes, said, "Ma'am,
I don't care if you think it's funny or not.
He's dead and it's the truth. Can we finish the roll?"
By then she decided we were out of line
and pink-slipped us to the principal's office,
where he lectured us on proper respectfulness,
and we left marvelling at how, even
when dead, Sandy got one over on us.
All during school we wanted nothing more
than out of there, to take our rock 'n' roll band
to the closest biggest town, but commencement night
we spent on Sandy's grave, and the next night
and the next. We couldn't pull ourselves away,
smoking and drinking in the tombstone shadows,
the night a chorus of aching cicadas, a wash
of laughter and feedback, a smattering of stars.
We howled with the dogs on the other side of the hill,
offered beer to the graveyard rats and possums
darting between the fence and plastic flowers
for a summer's worth of summer moons before
we let that bastard let us rest in peace.

Salem, Indiana, 1983

That summer my best friend Matt and I manned
the wheel of his father's 4WD red
pick-up through the fields and clumps of trees
and down the sudden turns of the Indiana
backroads to the family farm of his boyhood.
We loved the freedom of driving anywhere

and more the lie of speeding off to nowhere.
In the rush he told me his grandpa was a Klansman
one summer—how in all likelihood
Matt had found the faded, reddened
photograph of the last Indiana
lynching: a man hanging from a tree,

how it looked like the same slippery elm tree
he climbed as a kid, he didn't remember where.
A black family moved to Salem, Indiana,
and the neighbors descended on this one man,
flayed his skin from black to sticky red.
Matt's grandma sewed the white sheets and hoods.

He told me once how at a neighborhood
picnic his uncle took him under a shadetree
(It wasn't long ago, and Matt turned red
with shame.) and said, *We don't care where
they go. We have nothing against the Black Man—
We just don't want him here in Indiana.*

We finally made it to Salem, Indiana,
and as if to underlie the truth or falsehood
of Matt's story, there was the old man,

either sleeping or staring at the trees,
sitting on the back porch in his underwear,
his hair still a burnished copper red,

his arms and neck freckled and farm-reddened
from working the soil of the silty Indiana
fields. His socks were bunched and wrinkled where
they slumped below his ankles. I pictured the hood
over his nodding head, the whipping tree,
and dozing at his feet, the hatred for his fellow men—

another old fart in his underwear,
resigned to withering manhood, watching the red
sun burn below the Indiana treeline.

Reject

The summer we threw Reject down the pit
our hatred had been simmering all year.
We hated that he was always the first to laugh,
his way of standing hands in underarms
when we tormented him, and hated it
that mostly he was the only one of us laughing.
"Say it, Reject," we said, but he wouldn't say it.

Each time he refused we added to his sentence
until we'd piled up an ugly mouthful:
"Fat freckle-faced mouth-breathing faggot."
"Come on, Reggie," someone said, moved
by pity to use his real name. "Say it once
or they'll drop you down the pit." "Fuck you,"
said Reject, hands hiding a reddening face.

The pits were fifteen feet down, sink-holes
for ore and lead dug out with pick and shovel,
and altogether there were six of them,
walls only a few feet thick, like someone
had pulled a giant six-pack out of the earth,
though by now most of the holes have collapsed
into each other, the walls split by ravines.

After dinner we came back for Reject.
"Change your mind yet? You gonna say it?"
"Fuck you assholes," he said softly, not even
moving when the flashlight found him at the bottom,
his head resting on bent arms and knees.
"Okay, he stuck it out," someone said,
"Let's pull him up." We thought of his parents, worried,

his mom all blubbery with knots of Kleenex
wadded under her blouse, his dad behind
the meat counter at Big John's and who we called
the Jolly Butcher, surely not jolly then,
and we lowered the rope, but still he wouldn't look up.
"Just go away," he said to the rocky earth,
breathing in the dampness, shadows, and gloom.

"Come on, Reggie," we chorused from the edge,
but Reggie kept silent, vowing perhaps never
to join our overheated world at the top.
The rope wouldn't reach the nearest tree,
so we left it in a coil near the pit,
the bottom dark, untouched by a single moonbeam
and where we had no choice but to leave him.

Next morning we peered into an empty pit,
sucked on cigarettes stolen from our parents,
blew out excuses for our cruelty: as if
he had it coming, as if, like a salted slug
or hunted animal, he lacked the capacity for pain,
as if we were only being cruel to ourselves,
as if there were far less importance than meaning

in the world and all of us meant something different.
From the edge we looked into the sunlit hole
and wondered how he got himself out of there,
the coil of rope we left at the top untouched,
and the first beads of sweat began to bud
above our upper lips like phantom mustaches,
the day just starting to heat up again.

Under Your Bed

Was it so long ago that you believed
any body part was safe from my jaws
as long as it didn't cross the mattress edge?
But you soon learned my breath can make your mind
race on sleepless nights. As you lie holding
your lover, my poison tongue can hiss the names
of those who've shared this bed—unknown names too.
My scales creak in tightly wound bedsprings,
tweak your insecurity, and afterwards
echo *fake, fake.* But the worst I've saved for last.
With spiked tail I've wiped away these childish
aches and glamorous angsts, replaced them all
with something much more cruel and unimportant:
the dull pain I've planted in your back.

Phantoms

Because they couldn't find my father, a neighbor
had to drive Mother to the hospital.
And the week after I was born they snipped
the extra little fingers that sprouted between
my knuckles, like I had a smaller baby
growing inside of me, reaching out
along with my uncoordinated reach,
both of us grasping our mother's tearful face.

Looking closely thirty years later,
you can still see the marks left behind,
marks like alternate leaf scars on a twig.
But also, thirty years after doctors
pruned the tiny grasp within a grasp,
I can still feel those clinging phantom fingers.
I felt them through childhood piano lessons,
my ten digits plinking the keys, the tinier
ten playing a phantom counterpoint.
On the high school basketball team I felt
the spectral grip, guiding the ball through the hoop.
Together we struggled for every soft inch
up a girl's thigh in the back of my Dodge.

Later they trembled when I tried to dial
my father, my father who finally dragged himself
to the hospital three days after my birth
then fled forever from my deformity.
They quivered when I reached out to Mother
who folded herself in grief, like a beloved
tragic novel, and never did come out.
And now I not only feel those fingers

(in the firm, impersonal shake of a business deal),
I also see what must be the rest of that creature
when a shadow flits in the corner of my eye.

It happens late at night, when doing the dishes
or paying the bills. I look and there is nothing.
It has disappeared—flown in the radiator,
dropped down a crack in the worn floorboards.
My heart sinks, and I immediately lean
up the stairs to my wife, lying there reading.
And though I would never ever tell her this
(I couldn't bear bringing her to tears),
I know when I walk upstairs with a sunken heart,
and I feel the phantom twinging in my fingers,
that I could be going up to anybody,
that I'm only reaching out for anyone.

Mothra

Let's face it: I make a shitty monster. Moths
hardly instill fear in the hearts of man.
A cherry bomb could pound me back to powder,
and if the villagers only thought about it,
they could have simply built a giant bonfire
and I wouldn't have been able to resist—
I would have flown inside in a burning minute.

Did you know some moths have no mouths? They live
for seven days after sprouting wings,
time only to fuck, fly, and die.
Not me. I run at the mouth in my old age.
Now that my pupae have left the planet, I creep
down lonely streets at night, drawn to the few
windows not dark and shut but empty and blue.

Cyclops

I used to think the world was really flat,
that your second eye gave an illusion of depth—
a nymph near or far and my one eye wept,
and what's the difference between grabbing a fat
ewe and a cloud? I held them all in my palm.
Now, of course, I know the world is dark,
the fiery eye of the sun a snuffed spark.
The dance of color and shape has been embalmed
in memory and steeped in black skies
for this dark passage in which I fumble and creep.
I hear the scuttle of mouse bones in my cave.
The flutter of bats tells me when to sleep
while a murder of crows outside tells me to rise.
I wash in rocky echoes of the waves.

River Thing

I watched her through the sliding glass door
as she ate an egg and avocado sandwich
and sipped Chablis. Her husband away again,
I could smell her loneliness from across the field.
The scent of loneliness carries much further at night.
She must have smelled me too. I am so rich
and full this time of year with the moldering leaves,
the dank days. She looked up and saw me steaming,
slid open the door, stood aside, and I stepped through,
wordless and dripping. "You're like a warm mudbath,"
she laughed as I folded her into me. I nodded because
I have no mouth and caressed her with warmth and murk.
This week the banks will flood, and I'll take her,
the house, its very foundation, with me down river.

Pink Palace

Our ladders started in shit and stretched up
    to third-floor dormers as we scraped off the old
and slapped on the new: bright bubble-gum pink.
    The old coat looked like chewed-up wads of gum
that skulk along the bottoms of public pools,
    but Helen called the ramshackle Victorian house
The Pink Palace, and as we worked people
    drove by and yelled, "Jesus! That looks awful!"
We agreed and called it Pepto Abysmal.
    And as we coated and caulked, a yapping pack
of dogs streamed through the back door, refusing
    to let a single blade of grass grow
as they churned ammoniated mud that sucked
    our ladders deeper. Reglazing upstairs windows,
we glimpsed a lifetime accumulation of clutter:
    plastic milk jugs piled to ceilings, tin-foiled
tv sets in every room, and jumbled
    in corners, orgies of mannequin heads and limbs.
When cited by the city for refrigerators
    gaping in front and back and along the side,
fifty-year-old Helen came out in a pink
    terry halter and white short-shorts, eyebrows
painted archly, lipstick glittering, and stood
    cross-armed and turbaned like some Persian queen
as she upbraided bureaucrats and cops.
    Later that day, a man we'd never seen,
in his mid-thirties, emerged from the side of the house
    took off the door of each refrigerator,
stacked them in the alley, and went back inside,
    never to be seen by us again.
That summer hit a record 110 degrees,

and I don't know if it was heat or fumes,
but a Friday after lunch our boss collapsed
    by the front porch and sent us all home early.
I had a gig that night, the only night
    I didn't show up with pink fingernails
and forearms, and pink swatches in my hair,
    and as my girlfriend and I drove past the Palace
on the way to the show, I knew that everything—
    college, the summer's hasty romance, the rock-star
dreams I dragged behind me like some toddler's
    noisy pull-toy—was all a pile of shit.
But Monday morning we started earlier
    to beat the heat, and there we were again,
each of us on a different side of the house
    settling into the monotony of back
and forth, the brush zone, a long unbearable now,
    the vestiges of last week's pink daydreams:
Tom sees himself with full professorship
    never having to paint a house again;
Tiagon dumps his grad school scholarship
    and joins some backwoods Buddhist community;
and since the band sounded great on Friday,
    I see this cow-punk thing launching us out
of Evansville, Indiana, after all;
    each of us tallies the women we plan to screw.
And so we spread the third and final coat
    that Helen in her pink halter and turban
somehow twisted our arms to paint—wet paint
    gleaming, blinding pink, in the morning sun.

Prayer in Spring

At last the whores have taken back the park!
With most of us still bundled in our homes,
spring begins to strain in the buds and pull
our days at either end against the dark.
On street corners blackened ice and snow hills
have melted down to little gray gnomes.

And while my daughter finishes her homework,
brushes her teeth and waits for bedtime stories,
I walk our dog across the soggy sponge
of the park (stopping every few feet to jerk
his leash from new-thawed shit that makes him lunge)
and recognize one of last year's surviving whores—

a pretty thing, sweet, tall, but sad-faced,
and reminding me of a girl I knew and left
for someone else a dozen years ago.
At twenty feet I know her smell, her taste,
and despite "hey, want some?" I hop a patch of snow,
graciously declining her sad sweet gifts,

back to my daughter in her cherries pajamas
and offer, this one time in my life, a prayer—
that she will have the sense and security
when she outgrows my stories, these princely dramas,
to avoid all the men out there like me—
as she falls asleep beneath the story layers.

Us

We smile and hand your change across the counter,
sit at the next table in restaurants,
give you the correct time or polite response
in an elevator or some such brief encounter.
Some of us have married your closest friends,
even into your family, or perhaps you'll think
it safe to treat one of us to a post-work drink,
which is where this dance of masks always ends.
You let down your guard in the dim warmth
of happy hour. We push against our forms.
At first you can't believe what you are seeing.
Sometimes we also find you a bit revolting,
but here we are, across the table, molting
before your eyes into a human being.

Bar Poem

This poet walks into a bar, sits down,
and scribbles notes on a cocktail napkin.
The barkeep says, "Hey, you know we named
a drink after you?" "Really?" the poet asks,
suddenly looking up. "No, but we figured
you'd be self-absorbed enough to believe it."
What cheap cocktails might a poet inspire?
Fuzzy Navel Gazer? Arse Poetica?

Last night a bunch of poets got together
here and read their poems against the war,
not realizing that most Americans
would see a night like "Poets Against the War"
as a good argument for taking up arms—
if not against Iraq against the poets.
Before he died, one of my best friends
asked me, "How many poets does it take
to screw in a light bulb? Two. One to write
about the light, the other to gaze out
the window." He was a photographer and knew
about the light, and teased me that the only
light I ever wrote about was Bud Light.
After my friend died, his wife asked me
to write a poem for his memorial,
which I read in front of a couple hundred mourners.
I felt like a creep capitalizing
on a captive audience, on my friend's death,
catapulting my poetic career,
such as it is or ever could be. Poet!

At the bar there's a flyer from the "Poets Against
the War" reading. On the back someone
has written, "Oh shut up"—no doubt another
poet impatient to take the podium.
The lights dim and the bar grows crowded. Shadows
crawl up the walls, and the bar grays with smoke.
I tip an Arse Poetica to my friend,
to those about to die in the coming war,
which poets won't stop since poetry best
helps the living when honoring the dead.

Funeral Procession

Driving home from an autumn wedding,
the night's half-moon still fastened
to the morning sky, I thought I had
the highway all alone until
I caught the funeral procession,

each car marked with low-beams
and black flag snapping in the breeze.
I tried to pass before the lane
narrowed with orange barrels, forcing
me into their convoy, and suddenly

I, too, was a mourner, and I, too,
though flagless, put on my dims. We drove
in silent company for miles
beyond my motel, all of us caught
in this pageantry of death and marriage—

then the hearse veered down a farm road,
and the rest followed, tires billowing
yellow smoke, and I was flung
west, like ice-skaters crack the whip,
and my mourners would bury their dead

in six cold feet of Illinois silt,
and the trees would rake the last clouds
from the October sky, while I drove on,
sipping warm coffee, the morning sun
dissolving that last half-wafer of moon.

Slow Fires

Seen Burnt Prairie, Illinois? Where,
on either side of Highway 64,
oil wells have pumped through fifty years
like black chickens pecking mechanically
for a few splintered grains buried in the silt,
and the natural gas burns off the top
like a bonfire on a stick, only orange
and almost completely heatless. Sometimes at night,
weather conditions permitting, the fires bathe
the whole highway in an eerie, tepid dawn.
And if you think that's something, an hour west
can put you above the abandoned coal mines,
where fifty years ago a miner yelled
"Fire in the hole!" and that soft sulfur coal
never stopped raging underground. They say
the earth is hot enough to fry an egg,
but it could poach a whole cow strayed
from the field—that dry landscape, yellow and brittle,
where sheets of heat, like invisible sails
drift across the parched earth, following
the hellish fires that slowly gnaw its veins.
Sometimes you have to strain your eyes past
the bug-ridden windshield to find these slow fires,
past those scraps of forest across the fields,
past the isolated gas station rusting
to the pavement. Mostly you'd never know unless
you stopped a moment and heard it in the stories,
in the idle chatting, in the tone of the gas clerk
wishing you a pleasant trip right out of there.

Note on the Author

Born in Illinois, raised in Southern Indiana, and now living in St. Louis, Richard Newman is the author of three poetry chapbooks: *Monster Gallery: 19 Terrifying and Amazing Monster Sonnets!* (Snark Publishing, 2005), *Tastes Like Chicken and Other Meditations* (Snark Publications, 2004) and *Greatest Hits* (Pudding House Press, 2001). His poems, stories, and essays have appeared in a number of periodicals and anthologies, including *American Literary Review, Boulevard, Crab Orchard Review, 5AM, Meridian, StoryQuarterly, The Sun, Tar River Poetry, The Middle of the Middle West: Literary Nonfiction from the Heartland* (Indiana University Press), and many others. He earned his MFA at the Brief-Residency MFA Writing Program at Spalding University. He teaches at St. Louis Community College, reviews books for the *St. Louis Post-Dispatch,* and, for the last ten years, has served as editor of *River Styx.*

Printed in the United States
60475LVS00004B/115-117

9 781933 456010